THE CUB FAN'S BOOK OF DAYS

THE CUB FAN'S BOOK OF DAYS
A Guide to Every Year

By Jim Langford

Diamond Communications, Inc.
South Bend, Indiana

THE CUB FAN'S BOOK OF DAYS: A Guide to Every Year

10 9 8 7 6 5 4 3 2 1

Manufactured in the United States of America

Diamond Communications, Inc.
Post Office Box 88
South Bend, Indiana 46624-0088

Editorial: 219-299-9278
Orders Only: 800-480-3717
Fax: 219-299-9296
Website: www.diamondbooks.com

Library of Congress Cataloging in Publication Data

Langford, Jim, 1937-
The Cub fan's book of days : a guide to every year / by Jim Langford.
p. cm.
ISBN 1-888698-26-8
1. Chicago Cubs (Baseball team)--Calendars. 2. Baseball--Illinois--Chicago--Quotations, maxims, etc. I. Title.
GV875.C6L355 2000
796.357'64'0977311--dc21

99-052897

THE CUB FAN'S BOOK OF DAYS:
A Guide to Every Year

It may come as a surprise to some, but "longsufferingcubfan" is not one word. We are not so badly off as might at first appear. It may well be that we have watched more bad baseball than most, but every cloud has a silver lining and ours is that celebrated symbol of baseball named Wrigley Field. That is our meeting place, our Mecca, the center of gravity that draws generation after generation of fans and bonds us to the past, helps us endure the present, and urges us to hope for the future. Wrigley Field is home and Cub fans can go home again—as often as they wish.

Cub fans are not often understood, except by each other. Sportswriter and broadcasters, comedians and talk show hosts make it seem that loyalty to a team that hasn't won a World Series since 1908, or even been in a World Series since 1945, is equivalent to membership in a Love of Failure support group. In fact, we could categorize the barbs that come our way as follows: Cub fans must be really ignorant. They must really think the Wrigley Field is for picnics, checking out flesh in the bleachers, showing off a new cell phone, or working on one's suntan. In other words, Cub fans are simply uncritical.

Maybe it is that Cub fans are *losers*. We must like lurking in the shadows of last place. Remember the psychiatrist who analyzed the Cubs collapse in 1969 by saying that the Cubs (and presumably their fans) are literally afraid of heights and tend to panic when looking down from atop the division? I remember being asked in 1984 when the Cubs seemed well on their way to a World Championship, what team I would follow if the Cubs actually won it all. The implication, of course, was that it wouldn't be fun or chic to be a Cub fan anymore and we'd have to find a new logo to wear on our hair shirt so that we could continue suffering without losing a beat.

Or perhaps Cub fans are just *pollyannas*—such rosy-cheeked innocents and eternal optimists that the Cub reality, the actual record of their season cannot even begin to faze us. Were Cub fans even aware of the difference of an infield of Cox, Reese, Robinson, and Hodges with the Boys of Summer, as opposed to Serena, Smalley, Terwilliger, and Ward for our Busts of Summer? Do we really think that our current infield measures up to, say, Cleveland's?

I don't know whether I or any Cub fan can explain what draws and holds us to our team, but at least we can contest the misapprehensions that libel us and move on to this perpetual calendar that feasts in the face of famine and does so by bringing back memories of much more than wins or losses.

To the charge of ignorance, I respond "bull." Yes, there are some Yuppies, cell phone holders, and skin worshippers at Wrigley on any given day. But move around the park and listen to the conversations, sense the atmosphere in a tight game, listen to the response to a great or unusual play by either team and you will come to appreciate Cub fans. Don't mistake the ability to enjoy the total experience of a day at Wrigley as a lack of knowledge or concern about the intricacies of the game.

To the theory that we are losers because the team we support loses more games than it wins, I ask, since when is loyalty a disgrace? Anyone can be a fair-weather fan and a bandwagon booster. But real fans, real friends hang on through every crisis and disappointment. Such people are the opposite of losers. Jack Brickhouse used to say that if he were going into battle, he'd want to have Cub fans with him. Me too.

As for being pollyannas, let me point out that being tolerant is not the same as being indifferent or out of touch. We know perfectly well the difference between Atlanta's pitching staff and our own. But we also know that, on any given day, we can prevail. Hope is what makes the world tolerable. And the Cubs too. When we do win it all, you will see ecstasy, not bewilderment. We know the odds with successive casts of characters in the front office and on the field. Our steadfastness comes from a ballpark where we saw games with our parents and grandparents, to which we were wired from hundreds of miles away by radio broadcasts and telecasts that let us visualize what was happening on that glorious diamond. It comes as well from a kind of solidarity, of community, that we share. Most often we agree about who is good and who isn't, what we need and what we don't. Most of us remember where we were on that Sunday in 1984 when we lost game five to the Padres.

When I am in an unfamiliar place and I see a Cub hat, tee shirt, or bumper sticker, I feel safer, more at home. We may not be able to explain our allegiance to the Cubs, but we can and do share it, enjoy it, and measure our own history by it. This *Book of Days* is dedicated to the fans of the Chicago Cubs. May the memories be good, even if our teams haven't always been so. And may you record here your own new history from year to year so that the past merges with the present and toward a fabulous future.

JANUARY

There is something about the freshness of a new year. It is time to look ahead, to renew hope, and to be open to the unexpected in our life. But, even as we are anxious to move on, to forge ahead, let us not forget to appreciate who, where, and what we are in our life.

January has always been a time of optimism for Cub fans. Years ago, fans would wait for news of trades, study the spring roster for a phenom who would come from the farm system and stun the baseball world. There were some who flashed for moments or a month or a season, pitchers like Dick Drott, Glenn Hobbie, Bob Anderson, hitters like Bob Speake, Adolfo Phillips, Jerome Walton, and Dwight Smith. Now it is more a matter of free agent signings. With hired guns or not, the Cubs are bound to win it all some year. And that year, like this one, begins with January.

JANUARY

"Start by doing what is necessary, then what is possible, and before long you are doing the impossible."

—St. Francis of Assisi

NEW YEAR'S DAY

1

"In the long run, we hit only what we aim at."

— Thoreau

2

"All winter I sit and stare out the window waiting for spring."—ex-Cub Rogers Hornsby

3

"It's not wanting to be the best, it's *having* to be the best that makes a person into a superstar." —Billy Williams

4

"We love the Cubs because they are survivors and so are we."—Tom Dreesen

5

"Without heroes, we are all plain people and we don't know how far we can go." —Bernard Malamud

6

7

You can't steal second with one foot still on first.

8

"Dallas Green took on a task that would have given Hercules a hernia."—writer Ray Sons (1983)

"Real Cub fans are 99.44 percent scar tissue." —George Will

9

"Suffering is overrated."—Bill Veeck

10

"An optimist is one who believes a housefly is looking for a way out."—G. Nathan

11

"Cub fandom, like good looks and money, is inherited."
—Ned Colletti

12

13

1908 was the year Henry Ford introduced the Model T. It was also the last time in the twentieth century the Cubs won the World Series.

14

"Harry Chiti is the best kid catcher since Gabby Hartnett."—Cub general manager Wid Matthews (1955)

15

"Harry Chiti looked like everybody's brother-in-law. And played like him too."—Fred Harris

16

"Kids always chase rainbows; baseball is a world where you catch them." —ex-Cub Johnny Vander Meer

17

Don Zimmer's birthday (1931). Thanks for 1989!

18

"Every time I sign a baseball, I thank my luck that my last name isn't Peckinpaugh."—Mel Ott

19

"I wake up every day wearing Cub Blue. That's the way I like it."—Mark Grace

20

"As you get older, you learn that you have to make many more adjustments."—ex-Cub Andre Dawson

"The 1948 Cubs were the best ballclub ever to finish last in the National League." —General Manager Wid Matthews

21

"If a man can beat you, walk him."—Satchel Paige

22

"Any ballplayer that don't sign autographs for little kids ain't an American. He's a Communist." —Rogers Hornsby

23

"We don't care who wins as long as it's the Cubs!"
—Broadcaster Bert Wilson

24

"There are very few businesses that sell dreams. Baseball is one of them."—Bill Veeck

25

"There's a bit of Cub in all of us—a good deal of hope, lots of fear and excruciating loyalty." —Vince Lloyd

26

27

Cubs acquire Ryne Sandberg and Larry Bowa for Ivan De Jesus. (1982)

28

"We can win the pennant if the ball bounces right."
—Manager Charlie Grimm in 1960 (It didn't.)

"The essence of genius is to know what to overlook."
—William James

29

"I have never known a stranger—only friends I haven't met yet."—Jack Brickhouse

30

Ernie Banks' birthday (1931)

31

FEBRUARY

In the early years of the twentieth century, the Cubs trained at French Lick, Indiana, then in Southern California. Later when William Wrigley bought the team, Spring Training was held on Catalina Island which belonged to Wrigley. The last half century found the Cubs training in Arizona—(and pennantless.)

In the days before free agency, ballclubs were built on finding young phenoms, developing a productive farm system, and making shrewd trades. Every spring held out a special kind of hope that some young star would become a budding star, like Bob Speake did in 1955. His heroics took the Cubs to first place in May. With eight HR that month, five of them game winners, it seemed that for once we had the next superstar. But like a meteor his brightness quickly faded and by the end of the season he was back in the minors. Cub general managers spent their winters making trades in the hope that new faces would lead to higher places. Well after their primes we acquired or signed Robin Roberts, Lew Burdette, Goose Gossage, Dave Smith, Mel Rojas, Jeff Blauser, Ralph Kiner, Richie Ashburn, Don Hoak, Al Dark, Johnny Vander Meer, Dizzy Dean, the list could be endless.

Year after year, we lost ourselves in trades that often defied logic —Andy Pafko, Bob Rush, Bill Madlock, and, of course, Lou Brock.

Now, HoHoKam Park in Mesa, Arizona calls all Cubs and their fans to the yearly task of honing their skills and rekindling their hopes for one more run for the roses.

The sounds coming north—of baseballs hitting mitts and bats and fences—tell us that Spring will soon be here and once again our spirits can awaken and ready the call we have held in all winter long—GO CUBS!

"Hey, any team can have a bad century."
—ex-Cub manager Tom Trebelhorn

1

"You know that before you die, the Cubs are going to win it just for you. That's the way all Cub fans feel."
—Tom Dreesen

2

FEBRUARY

3

"If someone tells you he is a fan of both the Cubs and White Sox, check your wallet."—Jay Johnstone

4

"You cannot think that I enjoy being harrassed, riduculed, and maligned for being president of a last place team."

—P.K. Wrigley (1953)

5

"Chances of failure in baseball are always high. Cub fans somehow understand that. It's a higher level of baseball culture."—Roy Eisenhart, former president of the Oakland A's

6

"The Cubs may not be America's team, but they have been underdogs for so long that they are America's darlings."

—Harry Caray

7

"I don't like running. I believe in training by rising gently up and down from the bench." —Satchel Paige

8

"As a lifelong Cub fan, I've learned to tolerate and forgive almost anything. I've cheered outfielders who ran into the wall between innings, pitchers who fell on the mound and infielders who threw the ball to vendors."—Mike Royko

"Why Spring Training? Players do not need it. They come to camp with calluses and flat stomaches. Could it be that Spring Training is not for them, but for us?"—B. Lincicome

9

"I went through life as 'The player to be named later.'"
—ex-Cub Joe Garagiola

10

"I'm not going to be here next year if we lose big." —Cub manager Gene Michael (1987) (They did and he wasn't.)

11

"It is not conceivable that all the rookies will flop on us."—Cub manager Wid Matthews (1954) (Flop they did!)

12

LINCOLN'S BIRTHDAY

"It is not easy to do noble things without the proper equipment."—Aristotle

13

"In the 1970s the Cubs were like Rush Street—a lot of singles but no action." —Joe Garagiola

VALENTINE'S DAY

14

"There has never been a great athlete who died without knowing what pain is."—Bill Bradley

15

"The trademark of the old Cubs was to have clean uniforms."—ex-Cub Lou Brock

16

"For the old Cubs, 'run' was a word always followed by 'into trouble.' "—Phil Hersh

17

Harry Caray dies. (1998)

"I've found the next Willie Mays."—Cub manager Leo Durocher on Oscar Gamble (1969)

18

FEBRUARY

19

"Hope is the source of all happiness."—Philo

20

"We should have all our pitchers wear the same number; then we'll have at least one 20-game winner."—Actor and Cub fan Tom Bosley

21

"One loss is good for the soul. Too many losses are not good for the coach."—Knute Rockne

22

"Being a Cub fan is like being in limbo; paradise is always a day away."—Bryant Gumbel

WASHINGTON'S BIRTHDAY

23

"I ain't what I used to be, but who the hell is?"—ex-Cub Dizzy Dean announcing his retirement

24

"When I gave up a grandslam to [Cub] Pete LaCock, I knew it was time to quit pitching." —Cardinal great Bob Gibson

25

Andy Pafko's Birthday (1921), Ron Santo's Birthday (1940), Ed Lynch's Birthday (1956)

26

"The Cubs break your heart one day and have you wondering whether they'll ever win another game. And the next day they look so wonderful they have you floating in the clouds." —Cubs general manager Wid Matthews (1950)

"The one who complains about how the ball bounces is likely the one who dropped it." —Lou Holtz

27

Always borrow from a pessimist; he never really expects to get it back.

28

"Spring is the season of hope, especially for Cub fans. It is not as though we have forgotten the dashed dreams of the past, nor is it that we are so gullible as to buy the promises of the present. It is that we choose to hope against the odds, in spite of the obvious. That kind of hope isn't common these days but it sure is needed."—Bernie Lincicome

Jot down your hopes for the Cubs this year.

MARCH

1

Hoist one in honor of Harry Caray's birthday.

2

"I always thought a pat on the back, an encouraging word or a wisecrack paid off more than a brilliant piece of strategy."—Longtime Cub player and manager Charlie Grimm

"Never ridicule a beginner; you could kill talent before it develops."—Knute Rockne

3

"I deeply resent stories of what suckers the Cubs are."—G.M. Wid Matthews in response to critics of the Pafko trade

4

5

"It seems like just a short time ago Cub fans were excited about watching Carlos Lezcano roam center field and Lenny Randle play third. That was 1980. Hope was all a Cub fan had then." —Ned Colletti

6

"Sweat is overrated."—Cub manager Don Zimmer (1988)

Keep your head and stay smooth. All losing streaks eventually end. And so do winning streaks.

7

"Baseball is, above all, a matter of belonging, and belonging to the Cubs lasts a lifetime." —Roger Angell

8

"Don't mistake activity for achievement."—John Wooden

9

"Just a passing fancy."—P.K. Wrigley on night baseball (1935)

10

"To reach the port of heaven, we must sail sometimes with the wind and sometimes against it—but we must sail and not drift or be at anchor."—Oliver Wendell Holmes

11

"The number of players developed by the Cubs in the last 20 years can be counted on the toes of one foot."

—*Chicago Tribune* in 1958

12

13

"I know that once our programs are in place...we're going to win."—G.M. Larry Himes (1992)

14

"You have to be prepared for adversity; it's part of life." —Mgr. Whitey Lockman after he blew a 4-1 lead in the ninth (1973)

"When a flyball is hit, it should be caught. Otherwise it bothers our pitching staff."—G.M. Dallas Green after a bad exhibition game (1984)

15

"I've been trying to get Babe Ruth and Lou Gehrig but they aren't answering their phones."

—Jim Frey on possible deals (1989)

16

"All life is six to five against."—Damon Runyon

17

ST. PATRICK'S DAY

18

"From Roy Smalley I learned the meaning of the word 'overdue.'"—George Will

"If you refuse to accept anything but the best, you often get it."—W.S. Mangham

19

Dick Ellsworth's birthday. (1940)

20

"A team is only going to win so many games in a year. Why waste one in Arizona?"—George Will

21

RIGHT ON THE BUTTON DAY

"The Cubs are two players away from being a pennant winner—an outfielder and a starting pitcher."—Fergie Jenkins before the 1969 season

22

“Analyzing our team on paper, I think it is possible for us to take all the marbles.”—Cub athletic director Robert Whitlow in 1963 (Too bad we weren’t playing marbles.)

23

Ex-Cub Moe Drabowsky pitched for 17 years in six organizations and was known as a clever prankster. “My biggest prank,” said Moe, “was staying around 17 years.”

24

25

"We're creating role models here."—ex-Cub talent mogul Al Goldis (1994) (Did Al know something we don't?)

26

"We feel we're the team to beat."—Cub manager Tom Trebelhorn in 1994 (Apparently other teams had the same feeling.)

27

Cubs trade Bill Campbell and Mike Diaz for Gary Matthews and Bobby Dernier. (1984) Good Karma today!

28

"This I can say about the Cubs' pitching. A lot of it will be done from the stretch."—B. Lincicome

29

Manager Phil Cavarretta is fired during Spring Training for telling Mr. Wrigley the truth: that the Cubs have no pitching, fielding, speed, or hitting. (Phil was right: the Cubs finished seventh at 64-90)

30

Cubs trade George Bell to White Sox for Sammy Sosa. (1992)
Cubs trade Jose Vizcaino to the Mets for Anthony Young, the losingest pitcher in Met's history. (1994) This 38 years after trading Hank Sauer for Pete Whisenant.

"Older guys like to think everybody used to hustle, to play hard and smart. That's not so. We had lazy, dumb, careless players back then, too."

—ex-Cub manager and G.M. Jim Frey

31

APRIL

Opening Day. Life begins again. As much as we have been mesmerized by the long ball and enamored of slow-footed power hitters over the years, real Cub fans will confess quietly that what they want above all is pitching, with a mix of some power and speed to complement it.

The 1958 Cubs had five regulars with 20 or more homers and still finished fifth.

Even with sluggers Ralph Kiner, Hank Sauer and Ernie Banks in the same lineup, the 1954 Cubs finished seventh. Dave Kingman's 48 homers in 1979 could power the Cubs only as high as fifth. Even Sammy Sosa's 66 couldn't carry the Cubs all the way to the pennant.

Someone needs to get the message through to the front office that what the Cubs need is PITCHING, PITCHING, AND MORE PITCHING. We could win a pennant with pitching, speed, and defense—even in Wrigley Field. The fact is that the wind blows in more than it blows out in a season. And when it is blowing out, even a long fly is going to the bleachers. Somehow guys like Fergie Jenkins, Rick Reuschel, Maddux, Sutter, Sutcliffe, and, more recently, Wood and Tapani have been able to win at Wrigley. Do you really think Roger Clemens or Randy Johnson wouldn't have won with the Cubs?

Since 1945 we've tried everything but speed, defense, and pitching. We're ready. Go Cubs.

White Sox fans are such classy people!

APRIL FOOL'S DAY

1

If you need a helping hand, check the end of your arm.

2

Cubs trade Dennis Eckersley to Oakland where he becomes the best relief pitcher in baseball. In return the Cubs get Wilder, Guinn, and Leonette. (1987) Moral: Don't even take 3 for 1 today.

3

"Pitching is mind over matter, whoever the opponent, whatever the weather."—Fergie Jenkins

4

WGN's first telecast of a Cubs game, Jack Brickhouse at the mike. (1948)

5

"On Opening Day, the world is all future, not past."
—Lou Boudreau

6

7

"Experience is a tough teacher, it tests you first and teaches you later."—Lou Holtz

8

Willie Smith's homer wins 1969 Opening Day game.

9

"We can't all be heroes; someone has to clap." —Will Rogers

10

"I'm not in the game for the money; this is about the only thing in life I'm good at."—Mark Grace

11

"Always do right. That will gratify some people and astonish the rest."—Mark Twain

12

Tinker, Evers, and Chance play together for the last time. (1912)

"This is the place you think about when you're playing ball in the backyard as a kid."—Jim LeFebvre on Wrigley Field

13

Cubs buy Ted Abernathy from Cleveland; he goes on to be N.L. Fireman of the Year. (1965)

14

15

Lou Stringer makes four errors in his Cub debut. (1941)

16

"Say what you mean, but pick your spots." —Gary Matthews

Ryne Sandberg gets his first hit as a Cub. (1982)

17

Cubs send three players and $185,000 to the Cardinals for Dizzy Dean; he helps them to the 1938 pennant.

18

"The trick in this business is not to let a loss or a couple of losses get you down mentally. You've got to go home knowing you can bounce back." —Jim Frey

19

Cubs beat Reds, 7-6, in first National League game played at Wrigley Field. (1916)

20

21

Cubs get Fergie and Adolfo Phillips for Larry Jackson and Bob Buhl. (1965)

22

"Do not go gently into the season, Cub fans; rage, rage against the blasting of our hopes." —George Will

23

Cubs acquire Jim Hickman and Phil Regan from L.A. for Ellis and Savage. (1968)

24

You think you're having a bad day? On this day in 1987 Cub pitchers issued nine walks in one inning.

"The Cubs told me to work on my switch-hitting. I did and it screwed up my career."—Mike Tyson (1982)

25

Cub outfielder Jack McCarthy guns down three Pirates at the plate in one game. (1905)

26

27

Billy Williams' birthday. (1938)

28

"We may not have the talent some of the other teams have, but we do have at least six guys who come to play every day." [six?]—Cub manager Joe Amalfitano (1981)

29

"This could be likened to a masochist's daydream or waiting for a root canal."—Manager Tom Trebelhorn as the 1994 Cubs go 0-12 at Wrigley

30

"Roy Smalley is likely to become one of the greatest shortstops in history."—Cub manager Frankie Frisch (1950)

MAY

The real Cub fan refuses the blindfold and smiles at fate's bullets. Why? Because one year, maybe this year—or next—the wind will blow out only when we're at bat, opposing fielders will drop flyballs, misplay grounders, and ignore the cutoff man. Pebbles in the infield will deflect our routine outs and make them into doubles. All the games we have given away over the past decades will be given back to us. That is what transforms a good team into a team of destiny. And it's our turn!

"I went through psychoanalysis; it helped me deal with my Cubness."—ex-Cub Jim Brosnan

1

Mark Grace gets two hits in first game as a Cub. "I have to show I belong here." (1988)

2

3

"You can have money stacked to the ceiling, but the size of your funeral will still depend on the weather."—ex-Cub Chuck Tanner

4

Mark Grace, using Sandberg's bat, gets first major league HR. (1988)

5

"If you like your job, it should be fun."—A sign in the Cub locker room (1950)

6

Kerry Wood ties Roger Clemens' major league record by fanning 20 Astros. (1998)

7

"The promised land always lies on the other side of a wilderness."—Havelock Ellis

8

Keep Trying Day. Cub pitcher Bob Buhl gets a hit after making 88 straight outs. (1963)

9

Go for it even if your dream only lasts for a day. Elder "Bunny" White was the Cubs' Opening Day shortstop in 1962. He was never heard of before—or since.

10

"We have tried ex-Cub players and ex-Cub managers. The best protection we can give our managers is to advise them to get out of baseball."—P.K. Wrigley (1965)

11

"The first thing a Cub fan does in the morning is to check the wind."—Rich Schwab

12

Cub Sam Jones fans the side with the bases full to preserve no-hitter. (1955)

13

FAN POWER DAY. Fans wave signs saying "Double your pleasure, double your fun, sell the Cubs in '81." (And Mr. Wrigley did!)

14

"They still play a World Series, don't they? It's been so long I don't remember."—P.K. Wrigley (1966)

15

Don Cardwell no-hits the Cardinals in his first game as a Cub. (1960)

16

"Have one good year and you can fool them for five more."—ex-Cub manager Frankie Frisch

17

Cubs lose, 23-22, on Mike Schmidt's 10th-inning HR. (1979)

18

Ryno's record errorless streak ends at 123 games and 581 chances. (1990) Jackie Robinson plays at Wrigley for the first time. (1947)

19

"When you're concentrating on getting a hit, you won't see the ball. But when you're concentrating on seeing the ball, you'll hit it well." —Billy Williams

20

Rookie Ken Hubbs goes 8-for-8 in a twinbill at Philly. (1962)

AWARENESS DAY

21

"If I don't get this team back up there right away, I'll probably be gone by the middle of June."

—Manager Jim Frey, fired June 13, 1986

GO FIGURE DAY

22

Wrigley fires General Manager Bob Kennedy only to replace him with Herman Franks who proceeds to sell Rick Reuschel to the Yankees.

23

Cubs trade Willie Hernandez, later to win a Cy Young Award, for Dick Ruthven. (1982)

24

Cub Jamie Moyer hurls one-hitter for nine only to lose in the 10th. (1988)

Fergie Jenkins becomes seventh man in history to record 3,000 strikeouts. (1982)

25

Cub Dick Drott fans 15 Braves in 7-5 Cub win. (1957)

26

27

"If we ever get a hit with the bases loaded. I'm going to throw a party on Rush Street."

—Don Zimmer on Cubs slump (1990)

28

"The Phillies outfield is like Venus De Milo—no arms."

—Harry Caray (1990)

"If it's true that you learn from adversity, I must be the smartest S.O.B. in the world."—ex-Cub Gene Mauch

29

MEMORIAL DAY
Cub Frank Chance is beaned five times in doubleheader. (1904)

30

31

Cub Jeff Pico pitches a shutout in his major league debut. (1988)

DESIDERIUM

Though the shakey violets around you
may wither,
plant your Cub flag
and stand firm;
No swoon, no storm can rob you of
your hope.

Even if you hear that your heroes
scored fourteen runs and still
lost by two, stand by them.
No one promised you a rose garden;
settle for ivy-covered bricks.

Aim for the fences
even if you do
strike out a lot.
Always throw your fastball,
but also learn
to duck.

Forty years of waiting
is but a speck in
the cosmic flow of time;
a few more won't matter.
Remember, when all looks hopeless,
the game is never over
until the last man is out.

When you see ex-Cubs on
pennant-winning teams,
remind yourself that
they had their chance with us
and muffed it.

Take solace in the knowledge
that, whatever else can be said of you,
you didn't trade Brock for Broglio.

It is better to have swung
and missed
than never to have swung
at all.

Know that even if it seems
that your wheels have spun
for years and gotten you nowhere,
you can handle it!
A lesser being might yield to despair.
But not you.
You've been there.

You're a Cub fan!
You're the best!

—from *The Cub Fan's Guide to Life*
by Jim Langford

1

Randy Hundley's birthday. (1942)

2

"Youth movements are great if you are young."—Rick Monday on being released (1984)

3

"You ought to run your hardest when you feel your worst."—Joe DiMaggio

4

Bobby Bonds trips on the artificial turf in Pittsburgh and breaks a finger in his first game as a Cub. (1981)

5

The big tension on the 1966 Cubs was which Cub would lead the league in strikeouts. It ended in a tie: Adolfo Phillip and Byron Browne each fanned 133 times.

6

Don't blame fate for accidents unless you're willing to give up credit for a hole-in-one.

"Stay away from firearms and don't room higher than the second floor."—ex-Cub manager Frankie Frisch's advice to new managers

7

"It ain't braggin' if you can back it up."—ex-Cub Dizzy Dean

8

9

Banks homers three times but Cubs lose to L.A., 11-8. (1963)

10

Leon Durham steals home leading a triple steal against the Cardinals. (1984)

A Day to Remember. Fans chant Olé as Adolfo Phillips has four HR, eight RBI, and two diving catches in double win over the Mets. (1967)

11

It's fine to imagine yourself making a leaping catch at the wall—but once in a while see yourself as the hitter robbed by that catch.

12

13

"On Friday the Cubs had an offensive meeting and a defensive meeting. They should have held a prayer meeting."—*Trib* writer Joey Reaves after a Cub slump

14

"Homeowners along Sheffield and Waveland can rest easy: The Cubs' pitching staff left for Phildelphia last night."
—*Trib* writer Andrew Bagnato (1990)

FLAG DAY

BEWARE/TRADE CAREFULLY TODAY: Andy Pafko traded to the Dodgers (1951); Lou Brock for Ernie Broglio (1964). On the other hand, Harry Walker and Peanuts Lowrey sent to Reds for Hank Sauer and Frank Baumholtz. (1949)

15

William Wrigley sells Cubs to the Tribune Company for $20.5 million. (1981)

16

17

Cub Zip Zabel goes $18\frac{1}{3}$ innings in relief and beats Dodgers, 4-3. (1915) "I'll always be a Cub at heart."
—ex-Cub Andy Pafko

18

"God himself couldn't win with this team."—Don Zimmer after he and Jim Frey were fired in 1986

"It is a thankless, discouraging job trying to run a ballclub."—Phil Wrigley (1953)

19

Sosa leaves fans awestruck by homering onto the rooftop of a two-story building across Waveland. (1998)

20

21

Cub reliever Jim Brosnan sprains his ankle warming up and is carried off the field without facing a batter. (1957)

22

"A manager needs three things: a good memory, patience and being able to recognize ability."—ex-Cub mgr. Joe McCarthy

Ryne Sandberg's legendary two homers off of Bruce Sutter in one of the greatest games ever at Wrigley Field. (1984)

23

Ed Reulbach pitches 18 innings in 2-1 win over St. Louis. (1905)

24

25

Cub Augie Galan is first major leaguer to homer from both sides of the plate. (1937)

26

"Even though we lost 13 in a row, we showed a lot of character."—Cub pitcher Steve Trout (1985)

Critics yelp as Cubs sign Sosa to four-year, $40 million contract. (1997)

27

Mark Grace's birthday. (1964) Cub Joe Tinker becomes first major leaguer to steal home twice in one game. (1910)

28

"I believe the Brock deal puts us in a better position to make a run for the flag."—Manager Bob Kennedy (1964)

29

"I think the Cubs gave up on me a few weeks too soon."
—Lou Brock, leading the Cardinals to the 1964 pennant

30

Baseball is not as simple as it looks. Every game presents a huge variety of possibilities that have to be weighed by the manager and coaches. At the heart of it all is the ability to take calculated risks. On every pitch there is strategy in operation: the guessing game between pitcher and hitter, where the fielders position themselves, who will cover which base, how the wind is blowing, who is next in the batting order, who to warm up in the bullpen and when to bring him in. All of this goes on simultaneously, almost instinctively, and the fan is challenged to capture all or even part of it in one eyebite.

It is good to learn that even the best laid plans can run afoul to chance and circumstance. You'll see easy grounders elude fielders by hitting a pebble in the infield, you'll watch home runs blown into long foul balls by a sudden gust of wind, and you will see games won or lost because of a checked-swing hit or the mistaken call of an umpire. There are things in life that happen like that too. The best we can do is to rebound from them with grace.

Courage, anger, exhaustion, and exuberance are part of every game, as they are of every life. If you study the records, you will discover that individual stars may dominate a team, but team play as a whole is the crucial factor in the final standings. No team has ever won a pennant without good utility players.

Finally, be gentle in your judgment of the Cubs. It does us no credit to complain about our players because they are not as good as those fielded by other teams. Our protest must be directed toward the management, which either thinks that these guys are really good or that we won't care if they're not.

As Bert Wilson used to repeat time and again with two outs in the ninth and the Cubs trailing by half-a-dozen runs, "The game is never over until the last man is out." It goes on through the winter until it takes up where it left off the previous season. Baseball is a celebration of hope. That's why the season begins in the spring.

"If you're in a slump, it's almost as if you look out at the field and it's one big glove."—ex-Cub Vance Law

1

Sosa goes 6-for-6 and sets Cub record with nine straight hits. (1993)

2

"The sleeping Cub has changed into a roaring bear!"
—Harry Caray in 1984

3

INDEPENDENCE DAY
Cub Mordecai Brown pitches his fourth straight shutout. (1908)

4

5

SAD FACT DAY
Steve Balboni made more money in 1990 than Babe Ruth did in his entire career. Gary Mathew's birthday. (1950)

6

Cub pitches hold Pirates hitless for 12 1/3 innings, but Cubs lose, 5-4, in 20th. (1980)

7

Mitch Williams fans Kirk Gibson to beat L.A. "Kirk never dug in on me in the American League because back then I was wild." (1989)

8

Hank Sauer's homer wins the All-Star Game; Cub Bob Rush is winning pitcher. (1952)

9

"He calls for the curve too much. He can't hit it so he figures no one else can either."—Casey Stengel on ex-Cub catcher Chris Cannizzaro

10

Andre Dawson's birthday. (1954) "Look in the dictionary under 'leader' and there should be a picture of Andre Dawson."—Rick Sutcliffe

Phil Cavarretta reaches base five times in All-Star Game. (1944)

11

Ron Santo's single drives in winning run in the All-Star Game. (1965)

12

13

Cubs sign Robin Roberts as a free agent—16 years too late! (1966)

14

Steve Stone's birthday. (1947)

15

Cub Bill Madlock leads N.L. to 6-3 All-Star win. (1975)

16

"Power is fine as long as it's consistent. If it cools, you're in trouble because you keep waiting for the big inning that never comes."—ex-Cub manager Whitey Lockman

17

Jim Hickman's hit in 12th wins the All-Star Game. (1970)

18

Cub Bruce Sutter is winning pitcher in All-Star Game for second straight year. (1979)

Phil Cavarretta's birthday. (1916)
Ed Lynch resigns as G.M. saying, "We just never clicked." (2000)

19

Cubs trade Davey Lopes for Frank DiPino. (1986)
Cub president Andy MacPhail assumes Lynch's duties: "I'm going to get it done or it will kill me."

20

21

Cub manager Frankie Frisch fired; Phil Cavarretta becomes player-manager. (1951)

22

"Wrigley's boys were like Doublemint: they'd start with a rush, then go totally flat."—Edward Kiersh

23

Dick Drott fans 14 Giants in 4-0 win. (1957)

24

Leo Durocher replaced by Whitey Lockman as Cub manager. (1972)

25

"Trying harder when things are going poorly isn't the way to improve performance."—*The Mental Game of Baseball*

26

Cub catcher Clyde McCullough hits three HR, but Cubs lose, 4-3. (1942)

Manager Leo Durocher goes AWOL to visit stepson at camp. (1969)

27

Cub Lou Brock homers off of Ernie Broglio of the Cardinals. (1963)

28

29

Manager Phil Cavarretta pinch hits himself and grandslams to beat Robin Roberts, 8-6. (1951)

30

"It isn't against the damn law to pitch a shutout."
—Manager Don Zimmer to his pitching staff (1988)

31

Jack Brickhouse inducted into Baseball Hall of Fame. (1983)

AUGUST

In the ancient myth of Sisyphus, the hero is condemned to an eternity of rolling a boulder up to the top of a mountain knowing that as soon as he gets it there, the rock will fall back to the bottom so that he must begin all over again. Cub fans can relate to that. But decades of patience and grit have made us superior to our fate. Forget the June swoons, the collapse of '69 and the crashes of '84, '89 and '98. The law of averages owes us a dynasty. It's our turn to be atop the mountain. Let someone else play Sisyphus for a while!

"The reason we love the Cubs is that they are survivors and so are we."—Tom Dreesen

1

"Avoid running at all times."—Satchel Paige

2

3

Mike Harkey becomes the first Cub since 1972 to win 10 games in his rookie season. (1990)

4

Dallas Green's birthday. (1934)

"When Dunston takes his time and pats his glove I go, 'oh, oh, he's really going to burn it.' "—Mark Grace

5

"Why should dropping a flyball be such a big deal?"
—Dave Kingman

6

7

Keith Moreland charges the mound after being hit by Mets' Ed Lynch. (1984) (Where is Keith when we need him?)

8

No Mas Rojas Day. Mel, McRae, and Wendell traded to Mets for Lance Johnson, Mark Clark, and Manny Alexander. (1997)

9

Cubs beat Mets, 6-4, in first night game at Wrigley Field. (1988)

10

"The Cubs aren't that good. Anyone who says they are doesn't know much about baseball."—Mets pitcher Walt Terrell after Cubs sweep the Mets (1984)

"They've sure got some weird people in New York."
—Harry Caray from Shea Stadium (1990)

11

"Every time I stepped to the plate I couldn't help but feel sorry for the pitcher."—Rogers Hornsby

12

13

Lou Brock gets his 3,000th hit, a single off of Cub Dennis Lamp. (1979)

14

"I always got a kick out of using Wrigley Gum to help beat the Cubs."—Gaylord Perry

15

"If I was playing 3rd and my mother was rounding 3rd with the winning run, I'd trip her."—Leo Durocher

16

Cubs rally for four in the ninth to beat the Braves, 4-3, on Charlie Grimm Day. (1932)

17

Billy Williams gets 2,000th hit. (1971)

18

"A pitcher's attitude—his utter confidence that he has an advantage of will and luck and guts over the hitter—is almost as important as his stuff."—Bill Veeck

19

Cub Ken Holtzman no-hits the Braves, 3-0, before 11,033 at Wrigley (1969)

20

Jerome Walton sets modern Cubs record by hitting safely in 30th straight game. (1989)

Rick and Paul Reuschel combine for major leagues' first all-brother shutout. (1975)

21

Lee Elia fired as Cub manager; Charlie Fox takes over. (1983)

22

23

"Cub fans are passionate fans and they voice their displeasure. I can appreciate that."—Manager Jim Essian on being booed (1991)

24

Ernie Banks hits 512th and last HR, off Jim McGlothin in 5-4 Cubs win. (1971)

"A slump starts in your head and winds up in your stomach."—Billy Williams

25

Ron Santo's 2,000th hit is a three-run HR in 10-9 Cubs win. (1972)

26

Charlie Root posts 200th win as a Cub. (1941)

27

“I’d rather disappoint the President than disappoint a kid.”—Gabby Hartnett (who didn’t charge for autographs)

28

29

Cubs clinch the pennant but go on to lose the World Series to the Red Sox. (1918)

30

Cub Stan Hack gets his 2,000th hit, a single off of Preacher Roe. (1945)

31

"When the flags are blowing in, pitch to the flags. When the flags are blowing out, don't pitch."—ex-Cub pitcher Bob Buhl

CUBS BASEBALL IS...
Milt Pappas—one pitch away from a perfect game—only to have Bruce Froemming call "ball four." The umpire defended his call by asking, "How could I sleep at night if I called that a strike?" To which Pappas replied, "If that's the case you wonder how he ever sleeps."

It is "Hey, Hey" when homers were all we could hope for and "Holy Cow" when we had speed in the arsenal.

It is Bob Rush losing, 1-0, to the Cardinals because Rocky Nelson circled the bases while Andy Pafko argued that he had caught the line drive, not trapped it.

It's Bobby Del Greco, brought in for his good defense, making the error in his first game as a Cub that allowed three unearned runs and cost Bob Rush a 4-1 loss. It's Roberto Peña with three errors and three hits on Opening Day 1965 and his manager, Bob Kennedy, commenting, "It looks like we're going to have some excitement with this fellow."

Cubs baseball is Hector Villaneuva musing, "When I'm hitting, they say I'm stocky; when I'm not, they say that I'm fat."

It is the left-field bleachers saluting Sarge and the right-field bleacher salaaming the Hawk; it's K's for Kerry and Sammy's swing and smile.

Cubs baseball is always to love the game, if not the result, always to savor the sight, if not the score.

It is always to feel an unspoken alliance with any stranger whose bumper sticker reads, "GO CUBS."

1

Cub Cuno Barragan homers in his first major league at-bat. (1961) It turned out to be his only homer.

2

Cub Milt Pappas comes within one pitch of a perfect game. (1972)

Cubs win in last at-bat for the 16th time in 1984.

3

"This is no Cinderella team. This is one awesome ballclub."—Cub Dennis Eckersley on the '84 Cubs

4

Red Sox pitcher Babe Ruth beats Hippo Vaughn and the Cubs, 1-0, in the opener of the 1918 World Series.

5

"The Cubs are the victims of seven years of bad luck."
—G.M. Wid Matthews (1957)

6

7

Greg Maddux beats Reds in first Cub start. (1986)

8

Cubs purchase Ernie Banks from the Kansas City Monarchs for $10,000. (1953)

9

Cub Bob Hendley one-hits L.A., but loses as Koufax hurls perfect game. (1965) Andy MacPhail named Cub president. (1994)

10

Cubs drop out of first place after leading since Opening Day. (1969)

"The secret of managing is to keep the 5 guys who hate you away from the 5 who are undecided."—Casey Stengel

11

Incredible! Sosa hits 60th as Cubs overcome 10-2 deficit to beat Brewers, 12-10, on a Tyler Houston HR. (1998)

12

13

Sosa's 61st and 62nd help Cubs to another come-from-behind win over the Brewers. (1998)

14

This time Bob Hendley's 4-hitter beats Koufax, 2-1, on Billy Williams' HR. (1965)

15

Sammy Sosa becomes first Cub ever to hit 30 HRs and steal 30 bases in a season. (1993)

16

Cub Burt Hooten grandslams off of Tom Seaver! (1972)

17

Ernie Banks goes 0-for-3 in his first game as a Cub. (1953)

18

Ryne Sandberg's birthday. (1959)

"Momentum is overrated."—Cub manager Jim Frey (1984)

19

"The best day of my life was when I was born."—Sammy Sosa on his special tribute day at Wrigley Field (1998)

20

21

Cub Grover Cleveland Alexander beats the Braves, 3-0, in 58 minutes! (1919)

22

Cubs trade Dickie Noles to Tigers for a player to be named later—which player turns out to be Noles who is returned to the Cubs on October 23. (1987)

Sammy hits 64th and 65th but Cubs lose on Brent Brown's misplay. (1998)

23

Cubs clinch division title as Sutcliffe beats Pirates. (1984)

24

25

Sosa hits 66th, a 462-ft. blast in the Astrodome. (1998)

26

Ernie Banks gets 2,583rd hit in 2,528th and final game as a Cub. (1971)

Cubs win 21st in a row on the way to the 1935 pennant.

27

Cubs beat the Giants, 5-3, for Wild Card berth in playoffs. (1998) Gabby's homer in the gloamin' kills the Pirates. (1938)

28

Cubs beat the Pirates in the ninth to clinch the 1945 pennant.

29

"We went down with our best."—Leo Durocher on why he didn't use his bench in 1969

30

Joe McCarthy inherited the last-place Cubs of 1925 and built the pennant-winning Cubs of 1929. Fired the following year for losing the World Series to the A's, McCarthy won eight pennants and seven World Championships in 15 years with the Yankees. His 10 rules for success in baseball add up to a pretty solid philosophy:

1. Nobody ever became a ballplayer by walking after a ball.

2. You will never become a .300 hitter unless you take the bat off your shoulder.

3. An outfielder who throws back of a runner is locking the barn after the horse is stolen.

4. Keep your head up and you may not have to keep it down.

5. When you start to slide, slide. He who changes his mind may have to change a good leg for a bad one.

6. Do not alibi on bad hops. Anybody can field the good ones.

7. Always run them out. You never can tell.

8. Do not quit.

9. Do not fight too much with the umpires. You cannot expect them to be as perfect as you are.

10. A pitcher who hasn't control hasn't anything.

Babe Ruth and Lou Gehrig each hit two HR at Wrigley in 7-5 Yankee win. (1932)

1

Cubs whip Padres, 13-0, in first playoff game. (1984)

2

Cubs make third triple play of the season, with Bill Faul pitching all three times! (1965)

3

"I'd play for half my salary if I could hit in this dump all the time."—Babe Ruth on Wrigley Field

4

5

Claude Passeau pitches a one-hit shutout of the Tigers in the World Series. (1945)

6

Jim Frey becomes Cub manager. (1983)

7

SADNESS DAY: Padres win 5th playoff game. (1984)
"The greatest accomplishment is not in never failing, but in rising again after you fall."—Vince Lombardi

8

"Nobody died here. We'll bounce back."—Sarge Matthews (1984)

OCTOBER

9

Cubs buy Hack Wilson from Toledo for $5,000. (1925)

10

Tigers beat Cubs in seventh game of the World Series. (1945)

11

Stan Hack, Jim Gallagher, and Wid Matthews resign in Cub shakeup. (1957)

12

Glenn Beckert's birthday. (1940)

13

"There is always some kid who may be seeing me for the first or last time. I owe him my best."—Joe DiMaggio

14

Cubs beat Tigers, 2-0, to win their second straight World Series. (1908)

15

Dallas Green named Cubs general manager. (1981)

16

"A Cub fan's best friend is always tomorrow."—B. Lincicome

17

"Cavarretta should get a bonus for watching the Cubs every day this season."—writer Warren Brown in 1953

18

"Things turned around for us last year, but they turned the wrong way."—Jim Frey (1986)

"If we could have stayed away from the 13-game and 8-game losing streaks, there's no telling what we could have accomplished."—Manager Lee Elia (1982)

19

"And if the Titanic hadn't hit that iceberg, it would have been a terrific cruise."—Harry Stein

20

21

"You must try to generate happiness within yourself. If you aren't happy in one place, chances are you won't be happy any place."—Ernie Banks

22

"Baseball is a monopoly, intolerant of opposition and run on a grab-all-there-is-in-sight policy that is alienating its friends."—Adrian "Cap" Anson in 1900

Cubs trade Billy Williams to Oakland for Manny Trillo. (1973)

23

In baseball, as in life, good karma doesn't last forever.

24

25

Cubs trade Jenkins to Texas for Madlock and Harris. (1973)

26

"Baseball games on radio at night taught generations of kids the meaning of success and the inevitability of disappointment."—Curt Smith

Between 1946 and 1987, the Cubs lost 534 more games than they won.

27

"Summer was like being bashed across the bridge of the nose with a crowbar 90 times."—George Will on growing up as a Cub fan

28

The real test is to be steadfast when times are bad.

29

"You make your own bounces."—ex-Cub Keith Moreland

30

"We'll trade Madlock as soon as we can find someone foolish enough to take him."—P.K. Wrigley reacting to Madlock's demand for a $300,000 salary (1976)

HALLOWEEN

31

WRIGLEY FIELD MONTH

This venerable shrine to hope needs a few months every year to host only snow and silence. So, like an old vessel still seaworthy it can once again be a home to all—neighbors, travelers, old timers, and neophytes—who come to marvel at its beauty and be enveloped in its magic.

Its guest list is endless; this park has held them all close to the heart and waited with them for the ecstasy of ultimate triumph.

For now, the peace of winter is well-deserved.

One nice thing about egotists, they don't talk about others.

1

"I'm not ashamed of what we've done in 6 years here."
—Dallas Green on being fired (1987)

2

3

"Ex-Cubs never die, they just end up in the Playoffs and World Series."—Dennis Lamp

4

Ernie Banks named MVP for second year in a row. (1959)

Bert Wilson, radio voice of the Cubs, dies at age 44. (1955)

5

"Anger is a luxury a pitcher can't afford."—Steve Stone

6

7

Cubs acquire Rogers Hornsby for five players and $200,000. (1928) Hornsby averages .350 in four seasons with the Cubs.

8

"Ability may get you to the top, but it takes character to stay there."—John Wooden

"I'd rather ride the buses in Triple-A than be a lawyer."
—ex-Cub Tony LaRussa

9

"In the long run, we hit only what we aim at."—Thoreau

10

Jim Frey is named Cubs director of baseball operations. (1987)

11

Sammy Sosa's birthday. (1968)

12

13

Ryne Sandberg named MVP. (1984)

14

If you rise to the occasion when it counts, people will remember you.

15

Charlie Grimm, who played or managed in five Cub pennant years, dies in Phoenix, Arizona (1983)

16

"Be a Cubs fan. It is a reminder that faithfulness does not necessarily mean success."—ethicist Stanley Hauerwas

17

Cubs trade Oscar Gamble and Dick Selma for Johnny Callison. (1969)

18

Andre Dawson named MVP. (1987)

"Cub fans are, by consensus, the best in baseball."
—writer Riger Angell

19

Frey hires Don Zimmer to manage the Cubs. (1987)

20

"The Cub fan is the kind of guy who will tip the head waiter $20 and still get stuck near the kitchen."

—B. Lincicome

21

Cubs trade Guy Bush to Pirates for Larry French. (1934)

22

"It is hard to come here and preach patience in Chicago."
—Cub president Andy MacPhail

23

Hack Wilson dies penniless at age 48. (1948)

24

Don't let a bad day rob you of your sense of humor.

25

"One thing about the Chicago Bears. When their season starts, it sure takes the heat off the Cubs."

—ex-Cub Bill Madlock

26

"Nobody ever went broke betting against the Cubs after the 4th of July."—*Bleacher Bums*

27

"No one can make you feel inferior without your permission."—Lou Brock

28

29

Cubs trade Ken Holtzman to A's for Rick Monday. (1971)

30

"Check the magic of a winning season and there are always reasons beyond great talent."—Ned Colletti

UNTIL SPRING

"It breaks your heart. It is designed to break your heart. The game begins in the spring, when everything else begins again, and it blossoms in the summer, filling the afternoons and evenings, and then as soon as the chill rains come, it stops and leaves you to face the fall alone. You count on it, rely on it to buffer the passage of time, to keep the memory of sunshine and high skies alive, and then just when the days are all twilight, when you need it most it stops."

—A. Bartlett Giammati

1

In 1935, the Cubs rejected a chance to buy Joe DiMaggio from the San Francisco Seals for $25,000.

2

Cubs acquire Hands and Hundley from Giants for McDaniel, Landrum, and Rittwage. (1965)

3

Jose Cardinal becomes a Cub, traded for Jim Colborn. (1971)

4

Cubs trade Rich Nye for Boots Day. (1969)

5

Bad Deal. Palmiero, Moyer, and Drew Hall traded to Texas for Mitch Williams, Paul Kilgus, and Curtis Wilkerson. (1988)

6

Cubs trade Randy Hundley to Twins for George Mitterwald. (1973)

Cubs trade Lefferts and Carmelo Martinez to Padres for Scott Sanderson. (1983)

7

Cubs draft Jody Davis from Cardinals' system. (1980)

8

9

Cubs trade Bruce Sutter to Cardinals for Bull Durham, Ken Reitz, and Tye Waller. (1980)

10

Cubs trade Chuck Rainey for Doug Bird. (1982)

11

Cubs trade Ron Santo to White Sox for Steve Stone., *et. al.* (1973)

12

"The Cubs will come back for more. They always have come back. They always will."—Warren Brown

13

Fergie Jenkins' birthday. (1943)

14

Cubs get Jose Vizcaino from L.A. for Greg Smith. (1990)

DECEMBER

"I've known 3 players who have no apparent hitting weakness: Babe Ruth, Ty Cobb and Hank Edwards."
—Cub G.M. Wid Matthews (*Hank Edwards?*)

15

"Cubs Fever: Catch it and Die."—T-Shirts printed in 1981

16

17

BUST DAY. Cubs sign free agent Dave Smith. (1990)

18

"I don't, I'm not an outfielder."—Mitch Williams asked how he expected to replace Raphael Palmiero

19

"Well, Mr. Durocher is Mr. Durocher. What do you want, good taste or a good manager?"—P.K. Wrigley defending his hiring of Leo

20

Cub great Gabby Hartnett dies at age 72. (1972)

P.K. Wrigley announces the College of Coach concept. (1960)

21

"The Cubs have been going without players for years; now they're trying it without a manager."—A typical reaction to the College of Coaches

22

23

"Courage is resistance to fear, mastery of fear, not absence of fear."—Mark Twain

24

"The invariable mark of wisdom is to see the miraculous in the commonplace."—Ralph W. Emerson

Christmas wishes for peace and more pitching.

CHRISTMAS

25

"Everything that irritates us about others can lead us to an understanding of ourselves."—Carl Jung

26

In baseball, humility is always one play away.

27

"You can learn very little from victory and everything from defeat."—Christy Mathewson

28

"Baseball must be a great game to survive the people who run it."—writer Arthur Daley

29

"One of our subsidiaries had a very good year."—Tribune Co. (1984)

30

Resolve, yet again, to fly your Cub flag high.

31

NEW YEAR'S EVE